COLORFUL PLACE

MINDFUL STORY & ART FOR KIDS

By Jocelyn Fitzgerald, LMFT, ATR-BC & Heather McClelland, MSEd

Illustratated by Jocelyn Fitzgerald

www.Breatheartcalm.com

This book should not be used in place of medical or mental health services.

Colorful Place aligns with CASEL.com social-emotional learning standards for teachers, school counselors, and psychologists in the public school setting. Therapists, art therapists, mental health professionals, and kids will enjoy the art extension ideas provided. Parents, child care providers, and anyone who works with children will appreciate this book's simple language and friendly format.

Cover art, all interior art, and photography is by Jocelyn Fitzgerald.
Photograph of authors by Anniewerks Photography.

All inquiries about this book can be sent to the authors at: hello@breatheartcalm.com
For more information, visit our website: www.breatheartcalm.com

ISBN: 978-057881922-8

For bulk orders of this book, contact:
www. breatheartcalm.com
email: hello@breatheartcalm.com

BreatheArtCalm
Vancouver, Washington

This book is dedicated to...

...all the kids in my son Dax's 4th grade class.
Thank you for being so enthusiastic, kind, and loving toward all my stories and art.
Children are some of my wisest teachers.
Jocelyn

...my students and my family.
I am honored to journey with you.
Heather

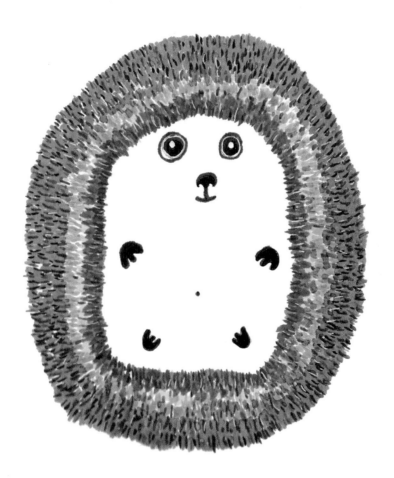

CONTENTS

Colorful Place

MINDFUL STORY AND ART FOR KIDS

INTRODUCTION

Why we wrote this book...

Children are dealing with more stress than ever in schools, online, and in society. In our work and in our daily lives, we witness children struggling with big feelings. Their struggles show up in the form of inattention, outbursts, anger, difficulty with peers, and more. Heather, a behavior intervention teacher, guides students to become more self-aware using the five senses and mindfulness. Jocelyn, an art therapist, teaches clients to use art to heal and regulate big emotions. We, as parents and professionals, found ourselves asking: How can we help children manage feelings in creative ways? That is why we created *Colorful Place*... for parents, teachers, therapists, and most of all, for kids.

What is a mindful story?

A mindful story blends being present to the moment with a relaxing, imaginative story. We can practice mindfulness by focusing on our five senses: tasting, touching, hearing, smelling, and seeing. The senses help anchor the body and mind to the present moment. This, in turn, can lower stress levels and rewire our brains to better cope with life's challenges. Breathing and counting are woven into the story to teach children how to practice calming techniques.

Why combine mindful story and art? They both...

Bring us to the present moment

Relax the body

Help us notice emotions in order to be more in tune with ourselves

Focus on process, not product

Art helps capture the essence of emotions beyond the reasoning mind.

How to use this book

An adult guides children on a mindful journey by reading the story to them. The story supports their learning about mindfulness with pictures and instructions. Coping skills are embedded in the story: breathing, counting, five senses, progressive muscle relaxation. Children practice these skills as the adult reads to them.

After the story, complete one of the suggested art activities. The art reinforces and furthers the skills developed in the story, making learning deeper and connections stronger. It makes the skills tangible and provides a concrete reminder of what was practiced in the story. We stop, pause, and look inward for direction rather than being concerned with a final product.

Ahead of Time

Create a welcome space

Find a quiet, distraction-free place.

Choose a spot—a couch, floor, or bed all work. Make it comfortable. Pillows and blankets help.

Enhance the experience with soft, relaxing music.

Engaging the child

This book is not intended to be used to de-escalate the child in the midst of big behaviors or feelings. Rather, this book invites the child to imagine and create. It should not be used as a consequence or to gain control of a child's emotions. If a child does not want to participate, try again some other time. Never force a child to participate.

Expectations

Expect wiggles and giggles. Don't be disheartened if your child won't sit still for the book or doesn't understand the story. Let the experience be what it is without passing judgment.

Mindful story is intended to be a practice—something you do over and over. Using this book regularly will help children notice and better manage their feelings and build stronger coping skills for life's challenges.

Finally, be aware of your own emotional state. Children learn by example.

Doing the reading

Review this book before reading with the child.

While reading, use your soft, calm voice.

Throughout the book, you will see [Pause.] instructions. Take as long as you wish for these pauses. A good starting point is counting to yourself 1-2-3-4-5 or in the reverse order. Some children might be very inattentive and will only pause for 1-2. The pause helps calm the body's nervous system.

This book can take as long as ½ hour if you stretch it out through longer pauses or take more time for questions at the end. Or it can take as little as 10 minutes if you skim read, pause quickly, and shorten the reflection questions at the end. Take the time that best holds your child's attention.

Try to build your child's stamina by practicing the book over and over to strengthen their mindfulness muscle.

Build a routine with the book

Before you begin, decide on the time: after breakfast, after school, or bedtime; and also on the place: on the couch, in a cozy corner, or outside, etc. Encourage the child to help make the plan.

Create a daily routine. Experiment—find out what time of day and what space works best.

MINDFUL STORY

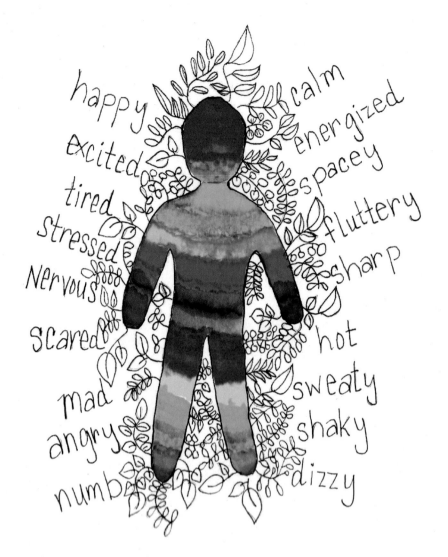

Take a moment to find a comfortable place to sit. When we notice what our body and heart are feeling, it helps us understand ourselves better.

Quietly to yourself, notice what sensations are you feeling in your body? [Pause.]

Silently, notice what emotions are you experiencing? What feelings are present? [Pause.]

Whatever you are feeling in your mind or body is neither good nor bad. Just notice it.

Imagine yourself in a safe, calm place. It can be a real place, somewhere you have been or an imaginary, pretend place. This place is peaceful and quiet. Feel a warm and gentle breeze blowing over your entire body, starting at your feet and going all the way to your head. Directly overhead and from beyond the sky, a warm sun shines down on you.

Let's focus on our breathing. When we focus on our breathing, our brain releases chemicals that naturally calm our body and mind.

- *Put your hands on your belly. Take a deep breath and fill it with air.*

- *Now let it out slowly and quietly.*

- *As you breathe, bring air in through your nose and out through your mouth.*

- *Notice with each breath how your body relaxes.*

- Let's breathe together. Breathe in through your nose, 1-2-3, and out through your mouth, 1-2-3.

- In through your nose, 1-2-3, and out through your mouth, 1-2-3.

- Continue to breathe slowly and let any stress or worries float away.

- We will count down as your body and mind calm down.

- You are getting relaxed... even more relaxed... deeply relaxed.

Imagine an orange and yellow sun warming your body.

- *You are going to be asked to tighten each muscle group one at a time. This will help your body learn how to relax.*

- *First, squeeze your eyes closed as if you're blocking out the bright sun and hold. [Pause.] Keep them shut.*

- *Slowly open your eyes. [Pause.]*

- *Now, lift your shoulders up to your ears, as if your shoulders can touch your ears and hold.*

- *Then let them relax back down, away from your ears. [Pause.]*

- *Think about your arms. Tighten your arm muscles by bringing your hands close to your chest. Squeeze your upper arms and lower arms. Hold and squeeze. Now relax the muscles.*

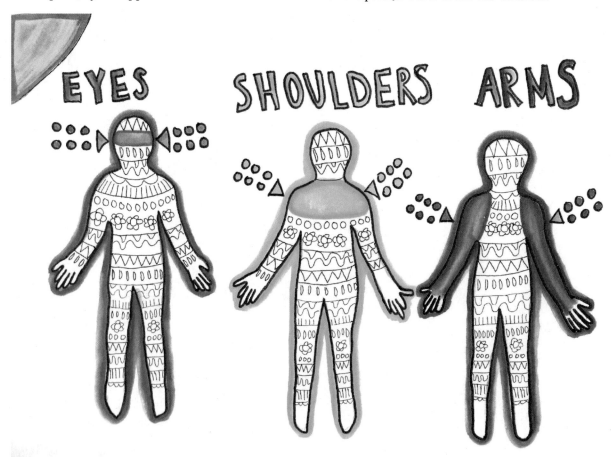

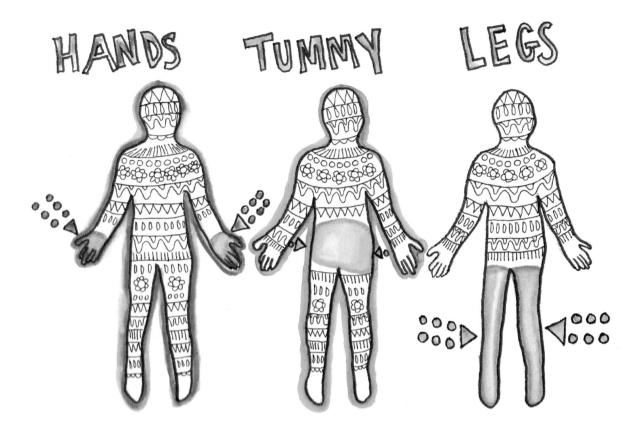

- *Squeeze your hands into a fist. Hold them tight. [Pause.] Now release.*

- *Squeeze all the muscles in your tummy by pulling your tummy in and holding your breath in for 5 seconds... 1, 2, 3, 4, 5. [Pause.] Now release.*

- *Make all the muscles in your legs tight. If your legs are straight, pretend they are long rays of sunshine. If your legs are crossed, make your leg muscles hard. Squeeze, squeeze. [Pause.] Now release.*

The next part of the story will be in your imagination. Wiggle around in your own space until you find the perfect position for relaxing. If possible, lie down or put your head on your desk. [Pause until settled.]

17

Close your eyes or keep your eyes open. Either is fine. Do what feels good and right for you. Use your imagination to create pictures in your mind as I read. Just like painting or drawing pictures in art, you will be using your mind to create the art of the story. There will be pauses to give you lots of time to paint a picture in your imagination.

Breathe in... and out... in... out....

You are creating a colorful place in your imagination. Look around. [Pause.]

See a field with swaying green grass. All you can see is bright green all around you. Gentle breezes are blowing over the field and you notice that your breathing is flowing with each breath of wind. The sun shines down on you as it glows orange and yellow. You feel so sleepy you lie down in the grass. You breathe in the green... and breathe out the green... in... out....

You notice that the sky above you is a bright blue with wispy soft white clouds. The clouds in your sky can be like the thoughts in your mind.... You see them as they float or drift by.... And again, notice the bright blueness of your sky.

What else do you see in your sky? [Pause.]

Look around the sky in your imagination. Breathe in the blue of the sky... and breathe out the blue... in... and out....

You are still in the grass and very relaxed. Arms are by your side. Your hands feel little soft purple flowers among the grass. You hold a velvety flower in your hand and gently touch each delicate petal. The petals feel like the soft fur of a puppy's ears.

You breathe in the purple... and breathe out the purple... in... and out....

You lift the purple flower to your nose and breathe in the scent of summer, sweet and calm. The sunshine warms the purple flowers, making the flowers' smell even stronger and sweeter....

Breathe in the sweetness of the flower... and out... in... out....

There is a bright red strawberry patch next to you. A small flock of birds are snacking on these perfectly ripe berries. You can't wait to taste the juicy red berries. When you do, you taste the sweet red flavors that burst in your mouth.

As you breathe in, you savor the tasty flavors of your wild strawberry... and breathe out... in... and out....

Listen to my voice as we go through all the colors in your colorful place.

- Rainbow colors are swirling around your body.

- Breathe in green... and out....

- Breathe in yellow and orange... and out....

- Purple... in... and out....

- Red... in... and out....

- The colorful mist flows around your body.

- You breathe in the colors of the rainbow and breathe out the colors of the rainbow.

- Stay relaxed.

- Take a moment now to notice all the colors in your imagination.

I will count back from 3 to 1, and then you will open your eyes.

Try to keep your body and mind quiet and calm as we come to the end. [Pause.]

Three, you are starting to wake up.

Two, begin slowly moving. Open your eyes if they are closed.

One, you are wide awake.

You're welcome to wiggle your toes and now your fingers.

If you are laying down or if your head is on your desk, gently sit up. [Pause.]

Slowly roll your head in a circle, starting with your ear to your shoulder. Then gently roll your head to the other shoulder.

Stretch both arms up to the sky.

Lean over to one side and then the other, stretching your arms as you lean and reach.

Roll your shoulders forward in small circles, and then roll your shoulders backwards.

What sensations do you feel in your body?

Do you feel the same or different from when we started the story? Why?

What did you see in your colorful place?

What feelings did you have when you visited your colorful place?

What part of the story did you enjoy the most?

Remember you can come visit this place anytime you need to relax. You have everything you need inside yourself to find calm. Let's review what we have practiced in this story:

Bring your attention to your body.

Relax from head to toe.

Close your eyes (or keep them open if you prefer).

Take a few deep breaths.

Count as you breathe.

Visit your imagination and paint pictures in your mind.

Notice each of your five senses: tasting... touching... hearing... smelling... and seeing.

ART RECIPES

SIDEWALK CHALK PAINTING
Time Needed: 30 minutes

Benefit:

Playing with sidewalk chalk paint helps to develop color recognition, sorting ability, matching skills, creation of patterns, and it strengthens the imagination.

Working with different sized spaces and different textures helps develop creative problem-solving.

Creating art in a public space, where friends and neighbors can see it, helps build confidence and pride.

Materials:

- 1 cup water
- 1 cup cornstarch
- 1 cup baking soda
- 5–6 drops food coloring
- bowls or squeeze bottles for each color of paint
- various paint brushes, sponges or squeeze bottles

Directions For Making Sidewalk Chalk Paint:

1. Combine water, cornstarch, and baking soda in a bowl. Mix it up until smooth.

2. Pour the mixture into separate bowls or squeeze bottles.

3. Add a few drops of food coloring to each bowl, enough to make the colors vibrant.

Discussion before Painting:

Close your eyes and remember the place you imagined in your mindful story. What part of the colorful story stands out to you.

Take a few moments to re-visualize your colorful place. What images came first to mind? What images or feelings are the strongest.

Pick one moment from the story to create a painting.

Discussion after Painting:

What scene were you drawn to? Why do you think that scene was your choice?

What colors were you drawn to? Why did you pick these colors?

Note: Painting on porous concrete may stick around longer than desired. If that's a concern, this paint also works great on dark-colored thick construction paper.

ABSTRACT AND 3-D RAINBOW ART EXERCISES
Exercise time: 15 minutes

Benefit:

Making art with primary colors eases us into a process of focus, concentration, and flow similar to the benefits of practicing mindfulness.

As we watch the colors mix and flow together, this exercise teaches us to slow down. We relax into the process because we are not attached to the outcome.

There's no pressure when we are just seeing how colors blend.

Materials:

- gallon-sized zip-sealed plastic bag or metal baking sheet pan
- white, flat, cone-shaped coffee filters
- spray bottle for water
- craft paper—white
- washable markers
- cotton balls
- glue sticks
- scissors
- pencil

Directions for Making Playful Abstracts:

1. Set coffee filters on waterproof surface (cookie sheet, large plastic bag). Using several colored washable markers, make silly designs.

2. Then, take the water spray bottle and lightly spray water onto the design and watch the color expand. Notice the new colors created where the colors blend.

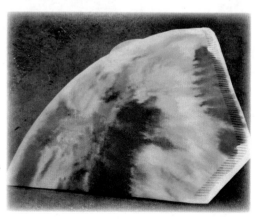

Directions for Making 3-D Art:

1. Trim the edges of the coffee filter so that it will lie flat.

2. Using a set of colored washable markers, follow the contour of the filter and layer the colors one after another creating a rainbow of colors.

3. Place the colored coffee filter on a waterproof surface and mist the colored circles with a spray bottle filled with water. Watch the colors blend and swirl! Set aside to dry.

4. Once dry, trim the filter away from the rainbow and glue the rainbow to white paper.

5. (Optional) Draw a face with a pen on the rainbow showing whatever mood you're feeling.

6. For a soft touch, use the glue stick to attach cotton balls around the edges of the rainbow.

Discussion:

What did it feel like to have no control over what the paint did?

What did you notice as you watched the colors flow together?

What colors stood out to you in the story? Are you able to see any of these colors in your art?

Think about what comes to mind and note what feelings you have when you think of each color of the rainbow?

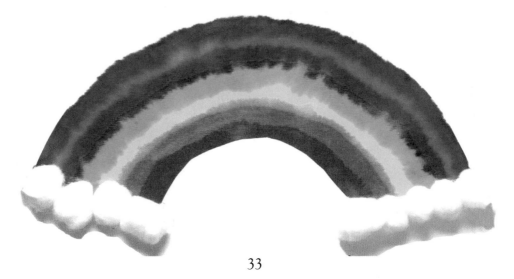

IMAGINATION COLLAGE
Exercise time: 50 minutes

Benefit:

Consider playing with each of the different paper types: colored tissue, colored construction, and magazine images.

This exercise increases relaxation and improves problem-solving skills.

Working with magazine images helps develop self-awareness.

The special benefit of collage making is that children who are never satisfied with their own drawing or painting can assemble a beautiful college using the work of others combined with their imagination.

Materials:

- poster board or card stock
- colored tissue paper
- construction paper
- glue
- magazine images
- scissors

Directions for Imagination Collage:

1. *With your child, decide on what type of paper you'll be using (or use all three to create a mixed media design) with your child.*

2. *Tear or cut sheets of different-colored tissue paper, construction paper, or magazine images.*

3. *Have fun moving around the different papers to create your artwork*

4. *When you're ready glue all your papers down.*

Discussion before Collage:

Close your eyes and see what parts of the story stand out to you.

Take a few moments to visualize images or feelings.

Pick one frame or moment from your "colorful place" to create a collage.

Discussion after Collage:

Once complete, take some time to share with someone what you created.

What colors were you drawn to? Why?

What feelings did you notice when tearing your paper up?

Note: Repeat this exercise from time to time. As your child matures, they may explore different parts of the story and want to try using different mediums. Make a collage without using scissors and another by cutting out different shapes. See what your child notices.

Drag, Scrape & Push Art
Exercise time: 30 minutes

Benefit:

This playful style of "process" art is fun for all ages. In a nutshell, process art means a child-led exploration of materials with no expectations of an "end" product. This project creates an abstract design that you can use as a launchpad for lots of other ideas. Once the child feels done, suggest stepping back and seeing what images appear in the art. One of the many benefits of this activity is that it helps to focus the child's mind on the here and now. By turning away from creating a perfect final product, the child has the space to play in color, design and texture, while being in the present moment.

Materials:

- *sturdy cardstock or paper*

- *paint: tempera or acrylic*

- *scraper options: old gift cards, combs, cereal box cut into squares or cut notches, kitchen tools (spatula, plastic knives, or forks). Don't limit yourself!*

- *wax paper or baking sheet*

Directions for Drag, Scrape & Push Art:

1. *Create a protected art play area by taping down a large sheet of wax paper on your chosen work surface. Then tape a heavyweight paper, such as cardstock, to the wax paper.*

2. *Apply 3-4 different colors of paint along one edge of the cardstock, leaving the rest blank. (See the picture.)*

3. *Spread the colored paints with a scraper. (See above.) Scrape starting from the side with the paint and spread it across the page.*

4. *Drag in straight lines, curve patterns or any design that suits your style.*

Discussion:

What did you notice in your body when you pulled the paint across the paper?

What sounds did you notice?

What were you surprised by?

What did you learn by using different tools?

About the Authors

Jocelyn Fitzgerald, board certified Art Therapist and Licensed Marriage and Family Therapist, and Heather McClelland, public school behavior intervention teacher, met when their children were in kindergarten. They soon discovered they shared a deep concern for children growing up during these anxious times. An idea took root and began growing. Combining their professional knowledge and skills, they envisioned something both practical and helpful, something that would bring together the calming, creative practices of mindfulness and art. Together, they completed Jon Kabat Zinn's Mindfulness-Based Stress Reduction (MSBR) course and peaceinschools.org "Mindfulness for Educators" training. They both live in the beautiful Pacific Northwest. Jocelyn and Heather have created a website dedicated to the mental health of children.

For more information about our products and other resources,
please visit us at our website:
www. breatheartcalm.com
email: hello@breatheartcalm.com

If you have enjoyed reading this book,
we would love for you to share it with others.
As authors, we are committed to making this
world a calmer place for children.

A portion of our proceeds will go to
Boys & Girls Clubs of America.

Made in the USA
Las Vegas, NV
20 August 2022